BISHOPS' CONFERENCE OF ENGLAND AND WALES

The Sign we Give

**Report from the Working Party on
Collaborative Ministry**

Acknowledgements

The Scripture quotations contained herein are from the New Revised Standard Version: Catholic Edition copyright © 1989 by the Division of Christian Education of the National Council of the Churches of Christ in the U.S.A. Used by permission, All rights reserved.

Extracts from the *Catechism of the Catholic Church*, English translation for the United Kingdom © 1994 Geoffrey Chapman-Liberia Editrice Vaticana, used by permission.

Extract from *Power Lines*, David Adams © 1992, published by Triangle, SPCK, Holy Trinity Church, Marylebone Road, London NW1 4DU, used by permission of the publishers.

Extracts from *All desires known*, © Janet Morley

Extract from *A Matter of Life and Death*, John V. Taylor © 1986, SCM Press.

Gather us in, Marty Haugen © 1982 GIA Publications Inc.

First published 1995

Published on behalf of the Bishops' Conference of England and Wales
by Matthew James Publishing Ltd. 19 Wellington Close, Chelmsford, Essex, CM1 2EE

ISBN 1 898366 14 4

Printed by Fraser Hamilton Associates, London

I have given them the glory you gave to me,
that they may be one as we are one.
With me in them and you in me,
may they be so perfected in unity
that the world will recognise that it was you who sent me
and that you have loved them as you loved me.

John 17:22-23

So in the Church the individual members do not live for themselves alone, but also help their fellows, and all work in mutual collaboration for the common comfort and for the more perfect building up of the whole body.

Mystici Corporis, Pius XII, 1943, n. 13

Since Vatican II, a new type of collaboration between laypeople and the clergy has happily come about in the Church. The spirit of readiness in which a great number of laypeople have offered themselves for the service of the Church must be counted among the best benefits of the Council. In this there is a new experience of the fact that we are all the Church.

Final Report of the Extraordinary Synod of Bishops, 1985, 2.C.6

Because of the one dignity flowing from baptism, each member of the lay faithful, together with ordained ministers and men and women religious, shares a responsibility for the Church's mission.

Christifideles Laici 15, 1989

We are convinced that the manner and style of relationships in the Church are part of the sign it gives, and for this reason we must develop patterns of collaborative ministry as a key feature of Church life to come. We wish to encourage all those, women and men, who have been trying to implement and explore such new relationships, with all their difficulties and promises.

Bishops' Conference of England and Wales, Reflections, 1993.

Foreword by Bishop Hollis

INTRODUCTION

A renewed way of being the Church

PART ONE

A Church in Mission: The context for collaborative ministry

PART TWO

Collaborative Ministry: Experience and theology

PART THREE

Collaborative ministry in practice

PART FOUR

APPENDIX 1

APPENDIX 2

Foreword

"We are convinced that the manner and style of relationships in the Church are part of the sign it gives and, for this reason, we must develop patterns of collaborative ministry as a key feature of Church life to come."

That sentence from the Glenridding Reflections of the Bishops' Conference has had a major influence in bringing to birth this report and the conclusions and recommendations that it makes.

The report addresses the urgent need that we have to establish patterns of working and collaborating in the Church – patterns which respect and cherish the essential dignity and consequent responsibility for the life and mission of the Church which belongs to every baptised Christian.

It has been my privilege to have been a member of the working party which has, under the very able direction of Pat Jones, produced this report.

We are not attempting to say the last word about Collaborative Ministry because that word will differ from community to community, and, in the end, such a word can only be written by those who participate in the process.

This is an attempt to encourage the Church at every level "to think more deeply and more imaginatively about the theology and practice of collaborative ministry."

It comes with the wholehearted approval of the Bishops' Conference and, if I may be permitted a personal reflection, I believe that it contains the seeds of a revolution in the way in which we live and work in the Church to-day. The revolution is not simply one which will affect radically our internal structures: it is a revolutionary insight into the way in which we exercise our mission, which is to proclaim the Good News in to-day's world.

✠ Crispian Hollis
Bishop of Portsmouth

A report on collaborative ministry

This report has been prepared by a working party of the Bishops' Conference of England and Wales, following a request from the National Conference of Priests. It is about some aspects of the growth and the potential of collaborative ministry in the Church in our countries. It explores collaborative ministry in relation to our experience and needs, at local, diocesan and national level.

'Collaborative ministry' is a term used to describe particular relationships, ways of working and patterns of ministry which bring together laypeople, religious, bishops and priests. These relationships and patterns are the practical implications of the vision of the Church expressed in the teaching of Vatican II and deepened in later documents. In part, they are a recovery of insights into the Church which have always been present in Catholic Tradition, but in another sense, they are new. They express what the Church is, and carry forward its mission in and for today's world.

Collaborative ministry is still emerging in the life of the Church. It has many different shapes and styles. It is influenced not only by our theology and faith, but also by our history and experience as a Catholic community in these countries and by our particular ecumenical, cultural and social circumstances.

The working party began with a basic conviction that collaborative ministry is a significant and challenging possibility for all of us who belong to the Church. The report reflects that conviction and explores both the theology and the practice which follow from it.

The final section of the report concentrates on five particular practical situations in which collaborative ministry is shaped. There are many others. These do not exhaust the scope or impact of collaborative ministry. In deciding to focus upon these five, the working party recognised the limitations of their time and experience. We also recognised that there are other groups working in areas that overlap with the task of this working party, and that we did not have to cover everything that could be said.

Reading and using this report

The working party intends this report to assist its readers to think more deeply and imaginatively about the theology and practice of collaborative ministry. It is offered in a spirit of dialogue to all those interested in its theme, and to those who are thoughtful about the future of the Church. It intends to be a helpful resource in preparing the ground for practical development. It does not presume that collaborative ministry alone is the way forward; but it stands firmly by the conviction that it is an inescapable element in whatever ways forward we find.

The working party decided to avoid making many recommendations. This is partly because pastoral priorities and plans are mostly decided at diocesan and local level. It is also because there are many different ways of understanding and encouraging collaborative ministry, and we wished to avoid suggesting any one model or strategy. However, we have added at the end a summary of some of the practical steps which seemed to us to lead towards collaborative ministry. We hope that these, and other ideas and suggestions of good practice found throughout the report, will stimulate imagination and encourage steps forward at all levels.

There will be many groups at local, diocesan and national level for whom the report will have interest and relevance. In particular, we hope that the National Conference of Priests will both discuss and use the report in their work, and commend it to diocesan senates or councils of priests through their members.

There is one specific recommendation to the bishops; that they consider asking priests and pastoral councils at all levels to read and discuss the report.

Language and limitations

The term 'collaborative ministry' is cumbersome. Some people dislike it, since they think it evokes negative associations. Others suggest alternatives, such as 'communion in mission' or 'covenantal working'. Like any newly arrived name, it can seem awkward at times. Nonetheless, many will recognise it as the most common name for the activity and theology this report explores.

In the report, we have used the term 'collaborative ministry' fairly consistently. But to give some variety, terms like 'working collaboratively', 'partnership in ministry' or simply 'collaboration' are also used at times. We recognise that some of these words carry different messages for different people, and convey varying shades of meaning. We hope that, overall, problems with language will not impede the main purpose of the report as a whole.

There are other difficulties with language in a report of this kind. It is cumbersome when speaking of various vocations within the Church to repeat a list of 'bishops, priests, religious, deacons, laypeople'. Yet each of these has a distinctive vocation and perspective on collaborative ministry. We hope that whenever the report speaks about laypeople, especially those working in pastoral ministry alongside priests, that religious involved in collaborative ministry will feel themselves included. We also hope that the general reflections in the report will be relevant to religious congregations who themselves are moving strongly towards greater collaboration.

Sometimes, we speak of 'laypeople', and at other times, of 'the baptised'. Language has limitations here also. 'Laypeople' has negative connotations for some, but is well understood. We use 'the baptised' as an equivalent and positive term, to refer to those who are fully initiated members of the Church. It therefore generally includes the gifts and mandate which confirmation celebrates. We also hope that, even where not specifically mentioned, all who belong to the Church, including black people, people with disabilities and young people, will feel themselves included. That is what we intend.

It is not possible to move very far forward into collaborative ministry without realising that language matters. The way we speak about each other reflects and forms attitudes and relationships. For this reason, we tried to take care with this report.

There are other limitations which arise from our decision to take a restricted focus. We decided to concentrate on some key areas, knowing that other areas of some importance would not be explored in this report. The most obvious of these is reflection on what happens when women and men work together in ministry, and how gender differences and expectations affect and enhance their collaboration. Another is the role of deacons in collaboration. Their role in enabling the development of collaborative ministry seems rarely discussed. It would also have been good to cover ecumenical thinking and practice more fully, to learn from the experience of other traditions. We became aware that in parallel with our working party, the Church of England had established a working party with a similar task, and although some exchange was possible, our two groups proceeded separately. Nonetheless we were grateful for the insights we gained into Anglican experience and practice, and hope that their report will be read by Catholics. Perhaps the next working party on collaborative ministry should be ecumenical from the beginning. We hope that as collaborative ministry develops, these further pieces of reflection will take place.

PART ONE

A Church in Mission:
The context for collaborative ministry

The influence of Vatican II

The Second Vatican Council gave the Catholic Church a renewed and dynamic understanding of its nature and purpose. It presented the Church as

> 'a communion of life, love and truth' and 'an instrument for the salvation of all; as the light of the world and the salt of the earth it is sent forth into the whole world'. (LG9)

Two of the most striking new emphases in all that the Council said about the Church are those which laid foundations for collaborative ministry; the emphasis on mission, and the recovery of laypeople's full share in the life, holiness and mission of the Church.

The Council documents spoke of the dignity and freedom of all the baptised and placed great emphasis on their primary mission to transform the world according to the vision of the Kingdom. But the documents also presented a renewed understanding of their participation in the life of the Church. The decree on laypeople affirmed that they have an

> 'active part of their own in the life and action of the Church. Their action within the Church communities is so necessary that without it the apostolate of the pastors will frequently be unable to obtain its full effect.' (AA 10)

The teaching of the Council has been further developed in Synod Exhortations, each exploring a different aspect of the Church's life and mission. *Evangelii Nuntiandi* spoke of the ministries of laypeople:

> 'the laity can also feel themselves called, or be called, to work with their pastors in the service of the ecclesial community, for its growth and life, by exercising a great variety of gifts and ministries according to the grace and charisms which the Lord is pleased to give them'. (EN 73)

These ecclesial ministries are

> 'capable of renewing and strengthening the evangelizing vigour of the Church'. (EN 73)

The theme of the Church as a communion, which was present in the central documents of Vatican II, began to unfold some years after the Council. *The 1985 Extraordinary Synod*, which was held to celebrate and re-affirm Vatican II, outlined the ecclesiology of communion which is explored later in this report and proposed that

> 'the structures and relations within the Church must express this Communion'.
>
> (Message to the People of God. Extraordinary Synod,1985)

That Synod also spoke explicitly about collaboration:

> 'Since Vatican II, a new type of collaboration between laypeople and clergy has happily come about in the Church... In this there is a new experience of the fact that we are all the Church.'
>
> (Final Report of the Extraordinary Synod. C.6)

Only four years later, *Christifideles Laici* expanded on Vatican II's call for participation, co-operation and consultation, and spoke explicitly of collaboration:

'...the recent Synod has favoured the creation of diocesan pastoral councils, as a recourse at opportune times. In fact, on a diocesan level this structure could be the principal form of collaboration, dialogue and discernment as well. The participation of the lay faithful in these councils can broaden resources in consultation and the principle of collaboration - and in certain instances also in decision-making - if applied in a broad and determined manner.' (CFL25)

Pastores Dabo Vobis then followed, presenting a theology of priestly ministry in the light of communion ecclesiology and speaking of the need for priests

'who are deeply and fully immersed in the mystery of Christ and capable of embodying a new style of pastoral life'. (PDV 18)

The Pope explains that to lead and encourage the ecclesial community, priests should have

'the ability to coordinate all the gifts and charisms of the community, to discern them and put them to good use for the upbuilding of the Church in constant union with the bishops'. (PDV 26)

It seems likely that the document from the most recent Synod in 1994 on consecrated life will extend this further.

The theme of communion has also given rise to a renewed and integrated theology of mission. It overcomes any separation between Church and world by proposing that the whole Church is to be intimately concerned with the world and deeply involved in its life precisely by living communion as fully as possible. The Church carries out its mission by living its own life, and this is the central way in which the gospel is proclaimed. As the Church lives communion, all people and all creation are drawn towards unity and community. This is the full meaning of collaborative ministry; not simply to renew the life of the Church, but to enable the Church to be part of transforming the world.

This support found within the Church's teaching documents has given inspiration and encouragement to those trying to develop collaborative ministry at a local level. It shows how the Church's thinking develops over time, and in relationship to new pastoral circumstances. There are still questions which have not been resolved in official teaching, some of which are explored in this report, but this too is part of how the Church continually searches for full faithfulness in its life and mission.

Pastoral development in England and Wales

Since Vatican II, much has been done to renew the Church according to the Council's vision. The Council's emphasis on baptism leading to shared responsibility and consultation has inspired new structures at all levels. The steady development of new roles and ministries open to laypeople has perhaps been the most significant factor in changing relationships and attitudes. Priests and people have gradually found that cooperation and collaboration is possible and fruitful. But this process of change has not been easy. There has been much resistance to these developments, and some have been wary or cynical about their implications. These attitudes still sometimes affect change in pastoral life today.

This is the full meaning of collaborative ministry; not simply to renew the life of the Church, but to enable the Church to be part of transforming the world.

13

There are some new developments which have been particularly influential in moving the Church towards collaborative ministry.

✤ One of these is the growing number of laypeople and religious employed in full-time pastoral work, usually alongside priests. This takes place in parish and diocesan pastoral teams as well as in retreat centres and various forms of chaplaincy work. The *Network for Lay Ministry*, started in 1991, now has 200 members, of whom it is estimated some 150 are employed full-time in a pastoral post. This report draws on their experience and insights in a later section.

✤ A new understanding of what a parish is, and new possibilities for ministry and leadership at parish level have grown gradually in many areas. An increasing number of priests see their ministry more in terms of drawing out the gifts of all rather than doing all the work themselves. Religious sisters and brothers have become more closely inserted into parish ministry, often working full-time in parishes. In many dioceses, permanent deacons work alongside priests. Parish missions, and programmes such as *The Parish Project* have helped parishes to generate a sense of shared responsibility for their life and purpose.

✤ A further new element is a focus on developing pastoral planning, or working towards an overall pastoral strategy. In some dioceses, much work has been done to produce parish, deanery or diocesan mission statements. Many dioceses have initiated a process of pastoral consultation, often culminating in a diocesan assembly or congress. Several dioceses have established diocesan pastoral councils in which laypeople and clergy work together to involve the whole diocese in exchanging ideas and setting priorities. In some places, these processes have been springboards for great activity. But there has also been frustration when their potential has been blocked by those who see no point in such work.

✤ The increasing adoption of the RCIA and other sacramental programmes have brought about new kinds of collaboration and new ministries. The RCIA in particular makes parishes more aware of the need to look at themselves and see how effectively their relationships and activities witness to their faith. It also introduces parishes to many of the basic principles and patterns of collaborative ministry.

✤ The impact of closer ecumenical partnership has made Catholic parishes aware that other Christian churches have strong traditions of lay ministry from which we can learn. These traditions also have different understandings of the role of leadership in relation to the community or congregation. Ecumenical dialogue has enabled us to contrast our own traditions and developments with other ways of organising Church life. This has had some influence on our own thinking and exploration, and promises more for the future.

These developments have gradually altered relationships and mutual expectations in the Church. In different ways, they have asked for revision of deeply embedded attitudes and assumptions about roles and responsibilities. They have sometimes caused conflict and tension, which has not always been easy to face. In a real sense, they have led the Catholic community into a process of conversion.

Changing pastoral circumstances

There are other factors which are part of the context in which collaborative ministry is growing. The number of priests is declining and their average age is increasing. This decline is not steep at present, but it will accelerate. For the next few years it may be masked by the number of former Anglican clergy entering Catholic ministry. However, it is also important to note that since Church attendance is also gradually falling, the ratio of priests to practising people is not significantly declining. This suggests the need to think about how we organise parish life with smaller and more disparate communities and what we do with our resources, including our buildings and money. Increasingly, we will face choices about which activities we want to maintain, develop or discontinue altogether.

Many dioceses have begun discussion about how to cope with fewer priests, and various different strategies are being adopted. Some of these are explored later in this report. Invariably such discussion rapidly identifies the necessity of involving laypeople more fully in parish leadership, in partnership with priests who may not even be able to be resident in the parish.

Whilst many stress that collaborative ministry should not simply be a pragmatic solution to a problem, others recognise that it is often practical pressures which bring about change. Whilst this may sometimes be true, it is not the best foundation for moving towards collaboration. If people do not desire to collaborate, or do not find that desire in those with whom they must work, directives or policy alone will not be sufficient for collaboration to work.

How the Church renews its life and mission

Collaborative ministry is not the only focus for growth or renewal in the Church today. Rather, it is one way of expressing how the Church renews itself. Some parishes and teams work to develop collaborative ministry very directly. But there are other significant areas of development in Church life and mission which also contribute to developing collaborative ministry, even if their primary focus is different. For example, some groups are working to broaden the participation of women in the life of the Church; others concentrate on developing networks of small groups or communities within parishes. Some parishes put their energy into particular priorities such as local community action or the RCIA, and let these activities gradually transform relationships and ways of working. Each of these can have a strong collaborative ministry dimension.

All these ways of pastoral formation and action overlap, and properly so, since they each express aspects of what the Church essentially is. But each one is incomplete on its own, and if pursued independently, could tend towards élitism

Change in the Church is ultimately the action of the Spirit, discerned through prayer and reflection as well as work and planning.

or sectarian attitudes. They all need the larger perspective of communion and mission, as well as continual exchange with other elements, in order to remain authentically ecclesial.

The process of growth in the Church is complex and variable. It happens in the interplay between various different influences, both theological and practical. Responding to the Church's official teaching is obviously of major significance, but development also happens when practical circumstances alter, including crises. The vision and commitment of individuals, whether bishops or laypeople, also bring about creative change in the Church today as throughout its history. And change in the Church happens in response to change in society and culture. Sometimes this means affirming values which society seems to be forgetting, or offering a critique of prevailing ideas. It also happens when the Church is open to new values or insights which societies and cultures propose.

Change is often unpredictable, and individuals and communities vary in their ability to cope with it. Change in the Church is ultimately the action of the Spirit, discerned through prayer and reflection as well as work and planning. It needs to be seen as the task of deepening our understanding of God's purpose and how we serve that purpose in and through the Church.

Collaborative Ministry: Definition or description?

Whenever people begin to talk about their experience of collaborative ministry, it becomes clear that whilst there are many common elements, there is no single model or pattern. The way in which it develops depends on the practical circumstances, the local culture, the age, gender, personal maturity and theological understanding of those taking part.

Rather than propose a definition of collaborative ministry, this report offers a description of the principles and convictions which shape it. These overlap, just as images of the Church overlap, but together they build a theological picture.

✤ Collaborative ministry is a way of relating and working together in the life of the Church which expresses the communion which the Church is given and to which it is called. It is a way of working in which the quality of relationships developed is as important as the task in which we are engaged.

✤ Collaborative ministry is an ecclesial activity; it brings together into partnership people who, through baptism and confirmation, as well as ordination and marriage, have different vocations, gifts and offices within the Church. It does not blur the distinctiveness of each vocation or gift. Rather it enables the identity of each to be seen and expressed more fully.

✤ Involvement in collaborative ministry demands conscious commitment to certain values and convictions. These include a recognition that Christian initiation gives us a shared but differentiated responsibility for the life and mission of the Church, and calls us to work together on equal terms; the conviction that our different vocations and gifts are complementary and mutually enriching; an agreement that we are accountable to each other for how we work and what we do.

✤ Collaborative ministry begins from a fundamental desire to work together because we are called by the Lord to be a company of disciples, not isolated individuals. It grows through a mutual process of conversion and formation. It also requires a willingness to face and work through conflict because of the attraction and value of a common good, supported by an awareness of participating in the work of the Spirit in the Church.

✤ Collaborative ministry is ministry committed to mission. It is not simply concerned with the internal life of the Church. Rather, it shows to the world the possibility of transformation, of community and of unity within diversity.

Exploring what ministry means: new ground for the Church

It is more difficult to define ministry than to define collaborative ministry. Since Vatican II, as ministries have expanded, there has been much theological reflection on the nature of ministry and ministries, but some key questions have not yet been resolved. The term 'ministry' is used in different ways and with varied understandings, in both pastoral life and in theology and Church documents.

Collaborative ministry begins from a fundamental desire to work together because we are called by the Lord to be a company of disciples

Ministry is rightly understood as the service based on baptism and confirmation to which all are called. In this sense, it overlaps with, and flows into, mission. It is the forms of life and activity through which the baptised express their discipleship, in the various areas of their life; home and family; neighbourhood and wider society; parish and diocese (CFL 59). The word 'ministry' has come to be used almost to signal that these daily activities are indeed mission.

'Ministry' can also be seen as some particular public roles or actions to which individuals are called by the Church and which they carry out for and on behalf of the whole body. Those who act as Eucharistic ministers, catechists and readers are usually the most visible examples of lay ministries. But there are other roles which some would argue should be seen in this light. These include teachers, school governors, bereavement helpers and others.

As this expansion and development of ministry and ministries takes place, some re-focusing of the essential role of the ordained ministry is inevitably needed. When the ministerial nature of the whole Church is more evident, it becomes clear how the ordained ministries have the distinctive role of serving, drawing out and unifying this ministerial character.

In this evolving situation, a number of questions arise;

- Which tasks are formal public ministries, and which are simply forms of service, spontaneously given?

- In which ministries should laypeople be formally commissioned, and why?

- Which ministries should have the more formal and stable kind of recognition known as institution, at present only available in Canon Law for lectors and acolyte, and then only for men?

- Why are Eucharistic ministers formally commissioned, but not catechists?

- What is the relationship between ministries exercised by the baptised, and the role of priests?

As long as these questions remain unanswered, there can be a danger of creating a two tier pattern of formal ministries and other ministries. The situation becomes even more complicated when lay or religious pastoral workers exercise specific ministries and take on leadership roles without any kind of commissioning, but with warm support from the communities they serve.

The documents of the Church do not yet provide answers to all these questions, but they do provide principles to guide development and reflection. Vatican II affirmed that the Church has many ministries:

> '(Christ) continually provides in his body, that is, in the Church, for gifts of ministries through which, by his power, we serve each other unto salvation so that, carrying out the truth in love, we may through all things grow into him who is our head.' (LG 7; also LG 12)

It also re-discovered the scriptural insight that all the baptised share in the one priesthood of Christ, that it is the whole Church that is a priesthood. In this context, the ordained priesthood can be understood more clearly. The Council laid out a guiding principle for the relationship between ordained and baptismal priesthood:

'Though they differ essentially and not only in degree, the common priesthood of the faithful and the ministerial or hierarchical priesthood are nonetheless ordered one to another; each in its own proper way shares in the one priesthood of Christ.' (LG 10)

Christifideles Laici took these principles as a starting point, and developed them further. In it the Pope emphasised that lay ministries, tasks and roles are gifts of the Spirit, given for building up the body of Christ. The Holy Spirit:

'lavishes diverse hierarchical and charismatic gifts on all the baptized, calling them to be, each in an individual way, active and co-responsible'. (CFL21)

The ministries laypeople exercise *'find their foundation in the Sacraments of baptism and confirmation'* (CFL 23) and *'exist in communion and on behalf of communion'* (CFL 20). They should be acknowledged and fostered by pastors (CFL 23), who should entrust to laypeople those offices and roles *'that do not require the character of orders'* (CFL 23). These include exercising the ministry of the Word, presiding over liturgical prayers, conferring baptism and distributing communion (CFL 23).

This recognition of the baptismal and spirit-given basis of ministries is very significant. It underlines that they are not privileges allowed to a few, but rather the natural outflow of the Church's life through the many. It is also worthy of note that the baptised may be given 'hierarchical gifts' from the Spirit. It is not yet clear what this might mean, but it offers a valuable principle.

Collaborative ministry, as it develops, cannot avoid the questions raised above. Indeed, it can contribute insights to the Church's continuing reflection on this matter by helping to clarify the identity of each vocation. It can deepen both the theology of ministry and the theology of priesthood.

The ecclesiology which underpins collaborative ministry

The working party found that reflection on collaborative ministry led directly into ecclesiological questions. We realised that whilst the language of communion ecclesiology is becoming familiar, and is prominent in current Vatican documents, its implications are often unexplored in the local Church. We found ourselves re-visiting our understanding of baptism, of the ministry of priests and bishops and of hierarchy, authority and leadership, in the light of communion ecclesiology and today's cultural and social context. The following section outlines some of the insights which give an ecclesiological underpinning for collaborative ministry.

Sharing in the life of God: the Church as communion

The central mystery of faith is the Trinity; the belief that God's very being is relationship (CCC 234). God is Father, Son and Spirit, a communion of persons. In God's own life, there is communion and relationship, distinction and diversity (CCC 255). But our faith in the Trinity is not just about who God is as God, but also about who God is for us. Trinitarian life is also our life, as we have been included as partners in God's own life. As human persons, we are made in the image of a God who is Trinity. The Catechism points out that this is not just an individual vocation but also a communal one:

> 'the vocation of humanity is to show forth the image of God and to be transformed into the image of the Father's only Son'. (CCC 1877)

It is in relationships, in our communion with each other, rather than in isolation from others that we will find fulfilment. We will reflect God's life if we live in this spirit of communion and collaboration and if our relationships are characterised by equality, mutuality and reciprocity. The vocation of the Church is to be a communion, a living source of Trinitarian relationships.

This is the basis for our equality in dignity as members of the Church and for our awareness of the spirit's activity within and between us. It is also the basis of the mission we share through baptism and confirmation. The Church, as Vatican II reminded us in the opening paragraph of *Lumen Gentium*, is to be

> 'a sign and instrument of communion with God and of unity among all people'. (LG 1)

and, as *Christifideles Laici* reminds us

> 'the Church knows that the communion received by her as a gift is destined for all people'. (CFL 32)

It is our mission to awaken persons to each other, to what their personhood means in terms of dignity and equality, and to express this in right relationships. (CFL 36, 37) In the public arena, this means building up participation and solidarity as the right basis for social and political relationships.

Implications for the Church's own life

Communion is the nature of the Church and the source of the relationships between all the baptised. Within its nature as a communion, the Church also has an order or hierarchical structure, which ensures its unity and faithfulness and fosters its spirit-given diversity. Both these together - the relationships and the hierarchical order - reveal the identity of each particular vocation. Within the communion of the Church, our different vocations are complementary; they enrich and complete each other. Each ministry and office in the Church, whether lay or ordained, serves communion.

The working party had two reflections on these theological principles:

✤ Our theology of baptism and of the Church as a communion is not yet sufficiently expressed in all aspects of pastoral life. There is a widespread sense that we do not yet use all the gifts we have to hand. There are also many aspects of our culture as a Church which still convey passive attitudes towards and from laypeople and or which expect those who are part of the hierarchical structures to compel obedience rather than invite conversion. The process of change is well-advanced, but there is still much to be done.

Let us love not in words or speech but in truth and action.
1 John 3:18, 4:7-12

Like good stewards of the manifold grace of God, serve one another with whatever gift each of you has received.
1 Peter 4:8-11

✤ A particular challenge is that of ensuring that our liturgy and sacramental celebration express this theology. This is why we need the fullest possible use of liturgical ministries. It is also why we need to think again about how to encourage more active responses from communities gathered for the sacraments. Those who do participate actively begin to discover this theology by doing so. For many others, it continues to remain a closed book.

Hierarchy in the context of communion

The theology of the Church as a communion is often presented as an alternative model to that of hierarchy. It is seen as a shift from a 'pyramid Church' to a 'circle Church'. This can be a useful starting point, but it also implies rather limited assumptions both about hierarchy and about communion.

It is true that some of the obstacles to developing collaborative ministry are attitudes which tend to be described as 'hierarchical' or 'clerical'. This usually means attitudes which over-emphasise the power and authority of those who are ordained at the expense of the rest of the baptised. But these attitudes also distort what hierarchy is and what the Church is.

As collaborative ministry develops, it brings about a renewed understanding of hierarchy, or at least recovers an emphasis in the meaning of hierarchy which is often neglected. There is a tendency to assume that hierarchy is a structure by which power is exercised over people. A renewed understanding would see it rather as a structure for ordering and unifying relationships and gifts, a service to communion. Hierarchy is what holds communion together, rather like the membranes in a leaf. It is part of what the spirit gives to enable the Church to be maintained in truth and unity. It exists in dialogue and tension with the wider consensus and varied voices of the whole body.

This renewed understanding of hierarchy draws upon principles laid out clearly by Vatican II. Both *Lumen Gentium* and *Christus Dominus* emphasise that office in the Church is primarily about service (LG 21,24,27, CD 16) and unifying (LG 23). In the recent letter about communion, the relational dimension of hierarchy is also emphasised; its task is

> *'fostering a unity that does not obstruct diversity, and acknowledging a diversity that does not obstruct unity but enriches it'.*

(CDF Letter on some aspects of the Church understood as Communion, n 15)

The working party offered three further reflections on the way hierarchy is understood:

✤ There is a tendency to confuse 'hierarchy', 'Church' and 'Bishops' Conference'. People often speak about 'the Church', when in fact they mean 'those who teach in the Church', generally the bishops. This can make the whole body of the Church, the body of believers, seem less important. There is need to encourage a more accurate use of these words.

✤ The principle of hierarchy is not confined to the Catholic Church. It is a feature of most Churches and Christian groups, and even seems to be more

...the body does not consist of one member but of many.
1Cor 12:14-31

rigid in some evangelical churches than in the most restricted Catholic interpretation. It is also present in secular organisations and is much studied in management theory. But a Catholic understanding of hierarchy differs significantly from secular interpretations. We see hierarchy in the context of communion, and as authorised and guided by the action of the Spirit. Both these vital theological principles should prevent hierarchy being simply an exercise of power and draw it towards ordering of relationships, unifying within diversity and discerning for the good of the whole body.

The Church's understanding of hierarchy before Vatican II was inevitably influenced by secular models such as monarchy and empire. Since Vatican II, we have begun to recover an older and richer theology of hierarchy. We need to take care that today's secular understandings do not replace the theological understanding of hierarchy outlined above.

✤ Although our theology describes hierarchy as a form of service, it is not always felt or seen as such. This is partly because many people approach it with the assumption that it is 'power over others'. Indeed, in the past, this assumption moulded attitudes, language and relationships in the Church. Many aspects of the culture of the Church still reflect this way of thinking impeding the growth of an atmosphere which supports collaborative ministry. We need persistent work to change these attitudes and assumptions.

Authority in the context of communion

The same kind of revised understanding is needed in relation to authority. Ultimately, all authority in the Church is from Christ, and is related to truth. But there are different kinds of authority in the Church, some arising from office or role, and others from personal experience or competence.

For collaborative ministry, two particular kinds of authority need recognition. There is the authority of all the baptised, expressed in their faith and witness, which Vatican II affirmed (LG35), and through which they play a part in the development of doctrine (DV8). There is also the authority of orders or office, exercised through teaching and in the pastoral charge of parishes and dioceses. Each of these carries a different kind of responsibility for the life and mission of the Church, and they are complementary. Ordered to each other, both should respond positively to the other. Collaborative ministry is a way of finding a harmony between these that serves communion.

When the communion nature of the Church is uppermost, authority can be seen in more relational terms. This means seeing how sacramental and theological aspects of authority, and juridical aspects, are complementary and need to be in harmony with each other. Authority is not a possession, but a relationship between the members of the body. The source of authority is its connection with the purpose of the whole body, the mission of Christ. Its primary power is power to enable, to call out gifts and to inspire mission, not power over people. It also safeguards legitimate diversity and identifies boundaries, so that the whole body can be faithful to its purpose.

Leadership which builds communion

Leadership in a Church of communion also needs to be seen in relational terms. It is not just a role or position, or a set of tasks. A leader who intends to express and build communion does propose plans and make decisions, and still holds ultimate responsibility, but includes people as far as possible in developing a vision, forming plans and making decisions. This requires a particular style of relating to people which is as consultative as possible.

The working party underlined two particular points:

✤ There is need for new images of leadership; the working party were attracted to the idea of the leader as the moderator of the aspirations and plans and priorities of the community, and the one who always holds the common good clearly before them. However, this may not always be practical. It could limit growth or change if this was the only kind of leadership given.

✤ In the experience of the working party, a strong lead from bishop or priests is one of the factors which most eases the path towards collaborative ministry. If bishops and priests model and teach collaborative ministry, it encourages and inspires people to develop confidence and conviction to move. We recognised the tension which exists here; collaborative ministry may need to be introduced strongly 'from the front' , so it can then develop in a collaborative way.

The role of the priest

In the light of communion ecclesiology and the reflections above, the way in which the identity and role of the priest is understood shifts. His pastoral and sacramental role remains vital, but with particular priorities. If his primary task is to enable communion to grow, rather than to 'run the parish', the relationships he develops will be central to his ministry. It is through the quality of relationships that he will most effectively invite people to make full use of their gifts and energy in ministries and other activities. He must be also able to let go of responsibilities and trust others with charge of various aspects of parish life and mission. In himself, he needs to be confident about a different kind of priestly identity with its source in the Trinity and its nature found in the *'interconnection of relationships'* (PDV 12) which make up Church communion. This is priesthood in which the *'fundamentally relational dimension'* (PDV 12) is decisive. As a servant of communion, he *'builds up the unity of the Church community in the harmony of diverse vocations, charisms and services'*. (PDV 16)

... a different kind of priestly identity with its source in the Trinity.

The need for priests who are committed to this perception of priesthood is crucial if collaborative ministry is to become widespread. The working party offered other comments from their experience:

✤ Many priests already understand their role in this way and express this in their ministry. However, others feel threatened by these new demands or ill-equipped to fulfil them. Some express willingness but prove unable to recognise the full implications or to change their basic attitudes. It is very difficult to know how to enable these priests to become aware of, and grow in, their inner understanding of themselves and their role.

❖ Priests, like bishops, can easily become the focus of the people's frustrations and resistance to change. New priests in parishes often have to meet and deal with negative feelings generated by their predecessors. It can be hard for him to propose new attitudes and ways of working when this happens. Priests and parishes need skilled help and support if they are to face these tensions and grow.

❖ One of the most painful experiences taking place in parishes and pastoral teams today is when progress is made, and then halted or reversed by a new priest arriving. There is an urgent need to look at how transition in parish staffing is arranged in order to respect what has been achieved in parishes and prepare the ground for good collaboration with a newly appointed priest.

The role of the bishop

It is in the ministry of bishops that the communion nature of the Church, and renewed understandings of hierarchy, authority and power, can become particularly visible and fruitful. His style of leadership and his proposals for diocesan life will give clear messages about what this means in practice. In particular, he can affirm patterns of collaborative ministry and give priority to structures and plans which make it possible.

An area in which it may be especially difficult, yet most important, for a bishop to express and invite collaboration, is in his relationship with priests in the diocese. If priests experience this relationship as expressing the values and attitudes of genuine collaboration, whilst still respecting the responsibilities of leadership, they in turn will be better able to do the same with laypeople. It is in matters such as how appointments are made, and how ideas and proposals are received, or decisions shared, that these values and attitudes most need to be found.

The working party offered these reflections from personal experience:

❖ Bishops can be placed in a difficult position in relation to helping collaboration to grow. They may want to promote collaboration by working in an open and consultative style, and yet the message they are given by some laypeople and priests is that firm leadership and decisions are needed 'from the top' to establish collaborative ministry almost as a requirement for all.

❖ The role of bishops is not well understood in today's Church. People tend to see the bishop as all powerful and the arbiter of all decisions. This is reinforced today by media stereotypes of bishops. But this does not reflect the reality of today's Church, and nor does it fit with our theology. Most bishops work with a range of officers, including laypeople and religious as well as priests, whom they have authorised to take charge of particular activities, taking whatever decisions are necessary.

Equal terms and equal valuing

The theology of communion implies a radical and true equality among all those who share in that relationship (LG32). This equality is based on what it means to be human persons and the dignity and integrity which follow. It incorporates diversity of vocation, role and activity. It does not mean that everyone is the

His style of leadership and his proposals for diocesan life will give clear messages about what this means in practice.

same, or must do the same work, but it does have implications for the relationships in which people work together and the ways in which varying roles and ministries are recognised and valued.

In collaborative ministry, there is a genuine need and desire to work together on equal terms. The extent to which this is possible depends on the practical situation. In a pastoral team, it becomes particularly important and must be reflected in decision-making and other aspects of how a team works. Across a whole parish, it is more likely to be a quality of relationships and structures within and between various groups and communities.

A sense of being on equal terms and of equal regard is vital in developing a culture of collaboration, and it is often hard to achieve. Working together on equal terms is difficult when one partner has more training, resources and recognition than others. It becomes more viable as laypeople build up experience and formation, although new difficulties can emerge when priests work with competent, qualified laypeople. Priests may feel threatened or inadequate alongside skilled or expert laypeople, and there may be tensions as both together learn how to make use of different skills and knowledge with mutual respect.

Tensions can also arise from different financial situations; when one is full-time and professionally paid, another is full-time but has living costs supplied and a very small salary, and others are voluntary, it can be hard to feel that there is equal valuing. Although the theology of communion implies equal valuing based on personhood and gift, we live in a world that measures value in other ways, and we cannot be unaffected by it. When priests and laypeople face this tension (and some may not), they need to explore what lies beneath and find deeper roots for their collaboration. They may also need to come to terms with financial constraints that limit what is possible.

There are some points which need to be kept in mind in relation to this matter:

✤ Working on equal terms, and indeed the whole of what collaborative ministry involves, does not in any way undermine the essential ministry of the priest. The identity of different vocations and gifts is not blurred by this way of working; on the contrary, they should emerge more distinctively.

✤ Equality has secular understandings related to individual rights and opportunities, which are very strongly held in today's western democratic cultures. Equality based on theological principles shares common ground with secular understanding but adds other elements drawn from communion. In particular, it requires a harmony between what is granted to individuals and the effects on the common life of the whole body.

✤ Some find the language of 'equal terms and equal valuing' puzzling. It is not always easy to be clear what it means in practice, as 'valuing' is often intangible. This is a struggle others in our society also face: how to create equal valuing whilst respecting difference, both personal and structural. It is interesting to note how the Equal Opportunities Commission has shown in

For by the grace given to me I say to everyone among you not to think of yourself more highly than you ought to think...
Romans 12:3-7

the field of employment that men and women may do work of quite different character but equal value. Our need of this principle in the Church is not for financial justice but rather to live communion, but we may nonetheless be able to learn from it.

Inclusive of all the baptised

The theology of communion, especially when expressed in today's cultural context, has an important message about inclusiveness. Communion means that unity can be found within diversity and that differences can be respected, and accepted as enriching and not divisive. In an important sense, to be inclusive is what it means to be catholic. In an increasingly fragmented society and world, the Church's ability to live as a sign of communion, and to draw out the implications for human relationships, is vital.

A communion Church is a Church which is inclusive of persons of all kinds, because of their unique personhood. It is a Church in which all are welcome and have a part to play, young and old, those who are disabled, black and white, men and women, rich and poor, lay, ordained, or consecrated. The relationships of communion are the new relationships of Christ, in whom

> *'there is no longer Jew nor Greek, there is no longer slave or free, there is no longer male or female; for all of you are one in Christ Jesus'*. (Gal 3:28)

To convey this effectively, the symbolic role of its ministry and leadership is very powerful. As many kinds of difference as possible should be represented in some way as a sign of the inclusiveness or catholicity of Church communion. Collaborative ministry is the most obvious and effective way of doing this.

The working party made the following comment on this matter:

❖ This is a difficult and sensitive area in the Catholic Church in England and Wales today. To take but one example, that of women; the Church's teaching, as recently restated by the Pope, is very clear that the Catholic Church does not consider itself authorised to open the priesthood to women. Yet in the cultural, political and economic life of our society, in which we must proclaim the Gospel, efforts are made to ensure that leadership is exercised by women, even to the point of quotas and strategies for positive discrimination. There is public outcry when a Cabinet is formed with no women, and senior ranks of education, the Civil Service and other major institutions are regularly surveyed to see how representative they are. Alongside this, the ordination of women in the Church of England has made the position of the Catholic Church seem very excluding.

Through collaborative ministry, the Catholic Church can show patterns of shared ministry and leadership which are consistent with Catholic teaching about priestly ordination and which include women, giving them a real share in leadership and decision-making.

Obviously, there are practical limitations to inclusiveness. There can be a tension between being inclusive and finding the right person for a particular

To each is given the manifestation of the Spirit for the common good.
1 Cor 12:4-12

role in a team. Nonetheless, collaborative ministry challenges us to open ministerial and leadership roles more widely, not simply for strengthening our own communion, but in order that we can communicate the gospel effectively in today's cultural world.

For Mission

As the Church becomes more deeply aware of the implications of living communion, the links between collaborative ministry and mission will emerge more clearly. *Christifideles Laici* reminds us that communion and mission *'interpenetrate and mutually imply each other'* (CFL 32). This partly happens in the outflow of living and experiencing communion in the Church. As people learn the values of communion already described, they take these values into their daily lives in family, work and wider society. This witness and action will often meet contradiction and opposition from prevailing social, economic and cultural habits of thinking, but there will also be affirmation and response, since these values are also held by others.

The very living of communion in the world is itself mission. The word that Pope John Paul II uses to make this aspect of communion clear is solidarity, the commitment to *'the good of all and of each individual, because we are all really responsible for all'*. (SRS 32)

Collaborative ministry has another kind of implication for mission which is as yet barely expressed. It offers a renewed way of supporting individuals and groups of laypeople active in particular fields of secular activity, and often feeling unsupported by the Church. As collaborative ministry grows, it can and should include and affirm those who work professionally in areas as varied as mental health, politics or other public spheres, as well as those involved in works of compassion and justice through voluntary activity.

The very living of communion in the world is itself mission.

PART THREE

Collaborative ministry in practice

Collaborative ministry: practical forms

When a parish is committed to collaborative ministry, this will become visible in the breadth of participation in all the ministries, tasks and roles of parish life, and in how they work together. These include:

Eucharistic ministers, parish council members, readers, catechists, teachers, school governors, youth leaders, group leaders, RCIA sponsors, prayer guides, bereavement ministers, AIDS befrienders and others.

It can also be expressed in a more focused way when the parish or deanery has a leadership team, in which laypeople or religious work full-time in pastoral ministry alongside priests. Full-time lay pastoral ministers often work in one particular field such as catechesis or spirituality. Examples of this kind of collaboration are:

parish pastoral assistants, parish and deanery catechists, full-time youth workers, parish administrators.

There are also pastoral teams who work in other settings and often make a strong commitment to collaborative ministry. These teams usually bring together laypeople and priests. Examples of these teams are:

diocesan Religious Education advisers or pastoral teams, retreat and pastoral centre teams, chaplaincy teams in Catholic schools and colleges, or in hospitals or prisons, seminary staff members.

In each of these settings, those involved in collaborative ministry face different challenges and questions, both theological and practical. They also need varying kinds of resources and support. Where a team lives as well as works together, collaborative ministry faces additional demands and tensions.

How collaborative ministry develops

Not everything that happens in the Church is collaborative ministry. There may be parishes with strong lay involvement but little genuine collaboration. There may be great advances in opening particular liturgical roles to laypeople, but without any change in parish structures or wider consultation in decision-making. Collaborative ministry does not happen just because people work together or cooperate in some way. It is a gradual and mutual evolution of new patterns, new attitudes and new self-understanding, which will not happen by accident. It must be chosen and consciously pursued from conviction. It will not work if those involved do not really want to do it, or feel it has been imposed.

The pace of development towards collaboration is influenced by practical circumstances. When there are few resources for formation, it slows down. When there is change in personnel, there can be a need to re-trace earlier stages, so as to move forward in new directions. The history and culture of the parish and neighbourhood also shape priorities and patterns of development. Parishes vary more in today's Church than in the past, and cannot all operate as one community. Collaborative ministry will be expressed differently in a northern inner-city parish, in a rural parish of a dozen villages or in a London parish with forty different nationalities. There is no single model of what collaborative ministry looks like.

Collaborative ministry does not happen just because people work together or cooperate in some way.

It must be chosen and consciously pursued from conviction.

Openness to change

Collaborative ministry asks those involved to be willing to change. Even when it is established and growing, it is vital that it remains open to further change. This is difficult; people prefer the security of familiar ground, and collaborative teams can become as fixed and exclusive in their new orthodoxies as earlier patterns, centred solely on priests, sometimes became. If collaborative ministry is to grow, the whole culture of pastoral life needs to become more positive about change and newness. The Church is a living and growing reality, in its pastoral structures as much as in its understanding and faith, and change is part of its nature.

Underneath this, there is a serious theological point. We tend to treat Catholic tradition only as something which happened in the past to which we must still be faithful today. But tradition is living and unfolding, in the present and in the future. De Lubac described it as follows:

> *'Tradition, according to the Fathers of the Church, is in fact just the opposite of a burden of the past. It is a vital energy, a propulsive as much as a protective force, acting within an entire community at the heart of each of the faithful.'* (De Lubac, p.91)

The eschatological dimension of faith calls us to be faithful to the future as well as to the past. Newness is a constant part of the Spirit's gift and presence in the Church, and we need not fear it even if we must discern carefully what it asks of us.

Pathways forward: some essential elements

Those who have experience of working collaboratively, both at parish level and in pastoral teams, describe its development as an intricate process. It has many elements, not all of which can be dealt with in a planned way. Some of these, such as learning to deal with conflict, must be faced when they happen. Others, such as growth in mutual trust and accumulation of experience, need to be allowed to grow in their own time.

Building mutual trust and recognition

Collaborative ministry is built upon good personal relationships. People who want to work collaboratively need a strong sense of their own identity and a desire for mutual trust and commitment. They must also be willing to move beyond fixed roles and stereotypes, to explore new horizons and to acknowledge their limitations and areas of vulnerability.

Mutual recognition is seeing others - whether bishops, laypeople or priests - as persons genuinely working to be faithful to the Gospel in their own vocation. It means discerning and appreciating that each other has the good of the Church and the Kingdom in mind, not the protection or pursuit of personal interests.

Sometimes relationships among those working collaboratively break down. It is caused by poor communication, misunderstandings, different temperaments, insensitivity and other human weaknesses. Priests and laypeople, men and women, are equally prone to behave in these ways. When this happens, whether

See, I am making all things new.
Rev 21:1-5

Newness is a constant part of the Spirit's gift and presence in the Church.

in a parish or in a team, a great deal of energy and time can be absorbed in sorting matters out.

For collaborative teams, where relationships are more personal than in the parish at large, this highlights the importance of emotional maturity as a prerequisite for effective collaboration. It also draws attention to the need for clear boundaries between personal and professional matters. The converse of these difficulties is that when relationships work well, they are tremendously empowering and affirming. They can create energy and enable growth.

Developing common vision and accountability

Collaborative parishes and teams generally place high priority on developing a shared vision, often expressed in a mission statement, or in regularly reviewed aims and objectives for their work together. This gives a strong sense of identity and assists them in being purposeful and disciplined in their use of time and resources. But it is important to see the development of a vision not just as formulating a static statement but rather as an understanding which evolves through reflection on experience and on the teaching of the Church as that also develops.

A shared vision implies a sense of mutual accountability within a team or a parish. This is not always easy for all partners in collaboration. It is unlikely that all priests will be familiar with planning their work or being accountable in this way. At the same time, it cannot always be tightly controlled, since so many aspects of pastoral work are unpredictable and spontaneous. It can also risk a different kind of exclusivity; a parish team may have a vision, aims and objectives, but this may not have been developed in partnership with the leaders and active members of the parish. The common purpose of collaborative groups, whether small teams or active parishes, should itself be discovered in a collaborative way.

Development of persons and skills

Formation and personal development are obviously important for those involved in collaborative ministry. Collaborative teams in particular need formation planned to meet their particular requirements as a team and not just a collection of staff. In addition, individuals should be encouraged to pursue their own personal and professional development, insofar as it is practical to do so. This is unlikely to happen without some moderate financial support.

Collaborative ministry needs particular skills. These are often learned informally, but they will develop more effectively if some training is available. Some of the skills used are relational skills, others are practical and work-related. Among the skills needed are evaluation, self-appraisal, listening, consulting, discerning, consensus decision-making, planning, group facilitation, and handling conflict.

Learning to deal with conflict

It seems to be almost inevitable that conflict arises within collaborative teams. Many people find conflict hard to face; some will prefer to deny that it exists or will smooth over differences without facing the issues underneath. If collaboration is to grow, conflict must be brought into the open. It can be paralysing when it remains hidden. The courage to face and work through conflict, negotiating until a compromise is found, and even seeking help in order to resolve it, are not weaknesses but signs of maturity and commitment. Collaborative partners can also agree to disagree, or to set aside areas where agreement or compromise cannot be found.

Shared decision-making

The desire for shared decision-making is a natural outcome of working collaboratively. It is an aspiration frequently expressed in the Church today, especially when thinking about how laypeople in general can participate more fully in the life of the Church. It runs the risk of becoming no more than a rallying cry if it is treated as an isolated aspiration. Shared decision-making in collaborative ministry is effective because it arises out of shared responsibility and vision, and mutual trust and recognition. It is these foundations which make it possible.

Many parishes and teams have developed a way of decision-making which is consultative in style. This form of decision-making brings wider resources to a decision than would be available to an individual alone. The more challenging option is aiming for consensus decision-making, in which the whole group or community works towards a consensus which becomes the decision. This may not be the decision that everyone wants, but will be one that everyone can accept, including those who may disagree.

In a small pastoral team where all the members are skilled and articulate, this is a fairly straightforward process. It is more complicated when the aim is to involve the whole parish in making decisions. The conditions which are needed for effective consensus decision-making to work are not easily found in a parish. They include:

- a shared vision;

- explicit and clearly agreed goals and parameters;

- an understanding of the process being used;

- a thorough understanding of what is at stake, including awareness of the Church's disciplines and teaching;

- skilled leadership;

- a consistent and limited number of participants, and adequate time for real dialogue.

These conditions are necessary within any organisation wanting to make decisions by consensus; within the Church, there will be two further elements which make the process ecclesial.

- It is important to order and weigh different kinds of contribution to the process: it is not a majority vote system, and not all voices are the same.

- There must be some awareness of voices that are unintentionally marginalised, or even missing altogether.

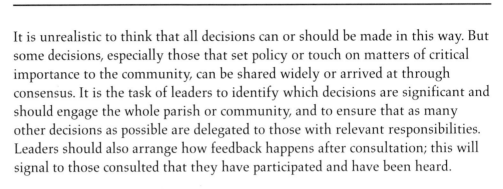

It is unrealistic to think that all decisions can or should be made in this way. But some decisions, especially those that set policy or touch on matters of critical importance to the community, can be shared widely or arrived at through consensus. It is the task of leaders to identify which decisions are significant and should engage the whole parish or community, and to ensure that as many other decisions as possible are delegated to those with relevant responsibilities. Leaders should also arrange how feedback happens after consultation; this will signal to those consulted that they have participated and have been heard.

Styles of meeting

Both in small pastoral teams and in parish development, working collaboratively will involve learning and using different styles of meeting in order to express in action the values and vision of collaborative ministry.

Some parishes and teams are familiar with at least two approaches: a business style of meeting, with agenda items, discussion and decision-making; and a formative style of meeting, in which there is dialogue and reflection on pastoral questions such as priorities for the parish, but little detailed planning. Collaborative ministry needs not only to use each style where appropriate, but also to combine elements of both styles, developing a way of working which harmonises them.

There are two other elements which are important:

✤ The first is giving time to discernment and prayer. It is vital that collaborative ministry does not simply become a system for running the parish; it must be overtly rooted in faith and God-centred, and it must take care to remain open and responsive to the world around.

✤ The second is recognition and use of people's expertise and energies. Meetings must be consistent in sharing out work and calling people to responsibility, rather than letting it drift back into the hands of a few, or even of one individual.

Liturgical celebration

This report has already noted that collaborative ministry needs to be made visible and celebrated in our sacramental and liturgical life. Here we describe the practical ways in which this can happen:

✤ Making full and inclusive use of all the liturgical ministries which are open to the baptised within the disciplines of the Church. (CFL 23) Laypeople can preside at funerals and at services of blessing, and lead liturgies of the Word, as well as taking on the more familiar Eucharistic and musical ministries.

✤ Occasional celebrations to recognise, commission or renew those involved in various ministries and activities help the whole parish to realise how fully ministry in the parish is shared. For example, the work of catechists or those who help with administration can be celebrated.

It is vital that collaborative ministry does not simply become a system for running the parish.

❖ More thought could be given to important moments of congregational response within liturgy. Too often these are passive murmurs rather than genuine symbols of shared responsibility. In the rite of ordination, for example, when the priest presenting the candidate to be ordained assures the bishop that 'enquiry among the people of God' confirms that this person is suitable to be ordained, there is rarely any symbol of how this has actually happened. RCIA liturgies, which often involve the sponsors or catechists visibly and audibly alongside the candidates in the various rites, offer new possibilities to explore. The importance of a layperson speaking on behalf of the community, in their own words, or the gesture of a group standing with candidates, goes some way to express wider collaboration.

❖ There are some important events in the life of the parish and of collaborative teams which should be celebrated liturgically. Such celebration affirms the collaborative pattern of ministry and relationships as a new ecclesial reality.

- When people from the parish are sent to, or return from, training for particular ministries.

- When a new priest is appointed to a parish, the induction should recount and celebrate the story of the parish and the relationships and ministries which make up its life, as well as welcoming a new pastor and listening to his story.

- When the parish or the priest reaches a particular anniversary.

- When a new structure such as a parish team or parish council is formed, or a new mission statement developed.

Creating a culture of collaboration

As collaboration grows, a different kind of ecclesial culture also evolves. Creating this culture is not, in general, an activity which is planned. Usually it begins to show itself in a gentle shift in atmosphere and sensitivity, expressed in attitudes and in many small signs. It becomes evident in the care that people begin to take with language; anything which stereotypes or diminishes either priests or others gradually drops away. It is sometimes indicated in how those working together address each other; formal titles may give way to more familiar or informal forms of address, and people are hardly ever arranged in hierarchical order, even at the top of meeting minutes. There is obviously a balance to be sought here between the familiarity of close colleagues and the level of informality which is appropriate in the broad life of the parish.

Such a culture may also be developed by the ways in which collaborating partners present each other and relate to each other when working in public. To see two or more people of different vocations working together and relating with equality and mutual respect is powerful for those whom they meet.

... a gentle shift in atmosphere and sensitivity, expressed in attitudes and in many small signs.

Barriers to growth in collaborative ministry

The barriers to the growth of collaborative ministry are the converse of many of the elements described above. It is important to recognise that these exist, and that collaborative ministry can as easily become rigid and confining as the more traditional patterns of ministry. Among the barriers which block growth are the following:

- Fear among priests or laypeople that collaboration will undermine priests or leave them with little to do. This may combine with a sense of loss of identity, especially as competent and qualified laypeople may be more successful in animating some aspects of pastoral life than priests.

- Financial pressures may mean that laypeople receive very low salaries, or frequently feel insecure about their own future, recognising that very few can be employed if proper salaries are paid. It can also mean that no money is available to pay for formation for laypeople. In addition, if priests have all they need to live reasonably well, but their lay collaborators feel insecure, tensions can result.

- The tensions that result when any members of collaborative teams fall into rigid behaviour or sectarian attitudes, rather than face the demands of making collaboration work. Sometimes teams have to face the hard question of whether it is possible to carry on with present membership if there is no real openness to change. The tension between being inclusive and being collaborative is sometimes painful and searching. There can also be tensions when some individuals become overdependent on other team members, or become very critical of authority in the Church.

- Stereotypes which trap people can be deeply embedded in attitudes in the parish. Some priests may be making great efforts to invite and model collaboration, and find themselves frustrated by responses which re-affirm unequal attitudes. Bishops also suffer from these stereotypes. It is not unusual, when conflict occurs, to see people who are otherwise collaborative asking for the bishop to 'do something', rather than working out a way forward together in the situation.

- Lack of continuity in parishes or teams; when a priest is moved, often a successor may not have been asked to take up the commitment to collaboration of his predecessor, and this can lead to loss and hurt within the parish. As parishes become collaborative, some system of enabling a priest to know what a new parish expects of him, and to respond, is urgently needed.

- Adversarial attitudes, often resembling those which are common in political and legal processes, which assume that the goal is winning a point or a battle, rather than finding the common good. Collaboration needs a spirit of dialogue and the habit of presenting opposing positions in the best possible light.

The tension between being inclusive and being collaborative is sometimes painful and searching.

Spirituality

Collaborative ministry draws deeply upon faith in the Trinity. It is not simply a way of re-organising work or structures. It is a way of expressing in our life together what God asks of us and calls us to be. It is therefore a spirituality in itself. Collaboration searches us, scrutinises our hearts and minds in the light of the Gospel and Trinitarian faith. It asks us to reflect what God is like in the ways we live and work together.

Those committed to collaborative ministry must open their personal and communal prayer to profound attention to what it means to receive and reflect God's own life. They must also connect this attentive listening to their daily experience, with its griefs and joys. Above all, they will need to let their prayer challenge them not to become inward-looking. The purpose of collaborative ministry is to enable the Church in mission. It must look outwards because God's life is for the whole world and all of creation.

Collaborative partners need to learn collaborative prayer. There is room for mutual spiritual ministry as well as pastoral care in collaborative working. Different attitudes to prayer and varying experience and formation need to be explored with sensitivity to what each can receive from others. Teams and partners need to work out together a pattern of prayer and shared worship with which all are comfortable.

Collaboration searches us, scrutinises our hearts and minds

Collaborative ministry: in five settings

Every situation in which collaborative ministry develops is different. There cannot be any fixed models of what it should look like or how it should grow. But it is possible to outline what it means to put collaboration into practice in various situations. The working party looked at five settings in which collaborative ministry can be pursued. Two of these - the parish, and full-time pastoral teams - are very obvious settings. There are already many parishes and full-time teams deeply committed to collaborative ministry. The others - seminaries, diocesan level pastoral planning, and strategies for a Church with fewer priests - are more difficult and complex areas in which to work out what collaborative ministry means.

The parish

What does a parish look like, if the parish as a whole is committed to collaborative ministry?

The decision to make a parish more collaborative needs to be made by priests and laypeople together.

The most important element is probably a shared vision of what the parish can be if all the members realise to the full their baptismal vocation and mission, both as individuals and as a community. The decision to make a parish more collaborative needs to be made by priests and laypeople together; both have to be willing to change themselves, rather than anxious to change each other. All those involved in leadership have to learn to share responsibilities, to trust others and take risks. They will also need to accept and live comfortably with decisions they may not personally have chosen to make.

In the early stages of this process, the example and encouragement given by the priest is vital; by his own attitudes and relationships, and more explicitly by his preaching, he can invite the parish to grow in this way. As it develops, it is important that in some way, a vision becomes explicit, so that all the groups, communities and organisations within the parish can feel it is their vision. The most practical tool yet developed to help parishes to develop such a shared vision is *The Parish Project*, a practical manual describing a nine month process that parishes can follow.

As it develops, a collaborative parish is likely to have the following characteristics:

Parish ministries

✤ The parish works hard to get as many people as possible involved in ministries and parish activities. This means not only liturgical and catechetical ministries, and also community action and work for justice. Those involved in each ministry see themselves as a 'ministry group' or team, working together in that aspect of parish life.

✤ Ministry groups take responsibility for their own formation, recruit new members, and assist those who have served for some years to move on and leave space for newcomers. A mature ministry group will coordinate and develop its own area of parish life, ensure good communication to the wider parish and community and handle its own budget.

❖ The whole parish understands what it means to be a parish of many ministries. They learn that no-one should take on more than one or two ministries, and that there is no 'pecking order'; all are valued. The liturgical life of the parish includes ways of recognising, dedicating, commissioning and renewing ministries.

Structures and decision-making

❖ There is a parish pastoral council or parish forum, which gradually forms a vision and learns to make parish decisions. A truly collaborative council or forum takes some years to build up, and needs formation in new skills such as making decisions by consensus. From time to time, the council or forum involves the whole parish in renewing its vision or priorities. It also tries to devolve as much responsibility as possible to groups and individuals.

❖ There is consultation with as many people and groups as possible in the parish on important matters such as sacramental policy, employment of pastoral staff and commitment to ecumenical projects. People and groups within the parish gradually learn patterns of consultation and decision-making, including awareness of the decisions in which they cannot all partici-pate, especially when confidential information is involved. They will also discover the criteria for communal ecclesial decision-making; the common good, rather than the interests of a group, and the perspectives of mission.

❖ There is openness about ideas and decisions. There is also good feedback on decisions taken following consultation to those who have been involved. People are encouraged to contribute ideas, suggestions and criticisms, through discussion in parish newsletters as well as in formal parish meetings.

Liturgy and culture

❖ There is liturgical celebration of the collaboration which takes place, in regular worship, and on special occasions.

❖ There is a sense of sharing and equality in attitudes and relationships, and an understanding that parish resources - buildings, people, money - are held in common and to be used in ministry for mission. An important symbol of this sharing is how parish property is used.

The Seminary

Pastores Dabo Vobis asks priests to embody *'a new style of pastoral life'* (PDV 12), and speaks of the fundamental importance of the priest having *'the capacity to relate to others'* (PDV 43). It also notes that it *'is particularly important to prepare future priests for cooperation with the laity'* (PDV 59). These emphases are echoed in the *Charter for Priestly Formation* in England and Wales:

> 'The view of the ministerial priesthood as ordered to the service of the common priesthood of all the baptised is essential in a Church which understands itself as communion... Formation for the priestly ministry must be a preparation for the exercise of this collaborative ministry through which the Church fulfils its mission to the world.' (Charter, n.30)

Collaborative ministry is not merely a subject for study in a seminary, although it has a theology. Rather, it is a perspective which needs to be present in many aspects of priestly formation, especially in the study of theology, and in pastoral and spiritual formation. Similarly, it cannot be just a set of ideas, but must be modelled in the life and practice of the seminary community. There are various directions that can be taken in seminaries to achieve this:

✤ The model of leadership which is visible in senior staff in the seminary needs to embody the principles of collaboration; openness to ideas, consultation of the whole community in appropriate matters, willingness to listen, commitment to building relationships, inclusion of people with varying gifts and experience within the seminary community.

✤ In relevant areas of theology, notably when studying the Church and the priesthood, current Church documents and writing about collaborative ministry should be well presented. In the study of philosophy also, valuable ideas about such themes as personhood, community and power can be explored. An integrated approach to teaching a variety of subjects also expresses the values of collaboration.

✤ Placements in parishes where collaborative ministry is well developed should be part of the pastoral formation of each student. The way in which placements are arranged should also reflect collaborative values; seminaries and parishes accepting students need a shared set of goals so that a placement is not just 'leasing' a parish for experience. Students should also play some part in formulating these goals.

✤ Parishes and pastoral teams with strong experience of collaborative ministry should be invited to contribute to the formation of students. The seminary's collaboration with diocesan agencies and other aspects of the wider Church should also demonstrate a commitment to this way of working.

✤ Seminary staffs should themselves gradually become more collaborative, with more religious and laypeople working alongside priests. As far as possible the relationships between and among staff and students should reflect the communion understanding of Church and a collaborative approach. A sense of shared purpose can begin to break down the insularity and individualism that are sometimes found in seminaries.

✤ Pastoral formation should include education in skills and processes relevant to working collaboratively, including decision-making, planning and facilitating, working with pastoral councils, and conflict resolution. It should also show the links between these practical skills and processes and the ecclesiology of communion.

However, even if a seminary is committed to these objectives, more complex difficulties remain, which touch upon sensitive areas of seminary life. The receptivity of students to collaborative ministry varies. They may have an idea of priesthood which does not reflect the communion nature of the Church very strongly. Some come with no experience of collaborative ministry. In assessing its students, seminary staff must both accept where they are, and ensure that they are able and willing to change. If seminaries are committed to enabling collaborative ministry to grow, they will need to incorporate the relevant criteria in their discernment and assessment of each student, as well as using methods of assessment which include mutual discernment. It should be clear before ordination that each student is capable of the relationships of mutual trust, recognition and collaboration with both men and women which will be expected of him in today's parishes.

Whilst seminaries have a vital role to play in introducing students to a collaborative approach to priesthood, it is not fair to expect seminary formation to achieve everything that is necessary. It is the whole Church which should form people for ministry. Seminaries need partnership with parishes and people who can extend and deepen students' experience and fundamental attitudes on these matters. Opportunities for some joint formation of students for priesthood alongside people preparing for lay ministry are among the most valuable ways in which this can happen.

Diocesan pastoral development

In the last ten years or so, most of the dioceses of England and Wales have under-taken some form of diocesan pastoral development. The pattern followed in each diocese is different, but usually involves one or more of the following elements:

✤ a diocesan process of consultation on particular themes, often using a discussion leaflet inviting people to meet in small groups and send in their responses;

✤ a diocesan level gathering, like a pastoral council or diocesan assembly, conference or congress, bringing together representatives from parishes or deaneries, religious and others;

✤ some feedback to the diocese, in a statement of vision or priorities, or resolutions, reported through the delegates at local level, backed up by the bishop and by a report;

✤ meetings at deanery or area level, either following the consultation, or following the diocesan gathering, to apply the themes discussed to practical local situations;

✤ initiatives to help the whole diocese to respond to the vision, priorities or practical proposals which have emerged.

Some dioceses work through a process of this kind once, then concentrate on implementing ideas at local level. Others have a continual cycle of consultation and meeting every one/two years or even more frequently. These processes are not the only way that diocesan pastoral development takes place. But since they are addressed to the whole diocese, and discuss its overall life and mission, they have a particular significance and potential.

It is the whole Church which should form people for ministry.

The fact that a diocesan process exists says to people that it is a collaborative community.

There are two ways in which diocesan processes help a diocese to move towards collaborative ministry:

❖ They provide an experience of a collaborative Church. They usually involve laypeople, priests, bishops and religious, meeting, working and celebrating together on an equal basis, contributing according to their different experience and roles. They often manage to reach beyond the constraints of tradition and expectation which can weigh heavily in some parishes. They can act as a symbol or message for the whole diocese. The fact that a diocesan process exists says to people that it is a collaborative community, sharing ideas and finding a common vision.

❖ They enable a gradual formation of ideas and attitudes across the diocese which provide foundations and resources for collaborative ministry at local level. They also teach people some of the skills which are central to collaboration.

It is worth noting some of the lessons which have been learned from experience of these diocesan processes, and which shed light on the development of collaborative ministry.

❖ These processes need visible leadership, involvement and encouragement from the bishop; when this happens, the level of motivation is very high. They also have to cope with people's expectations, which can become unrealistic, and their frustrations and even anger from the past. These are healthy parts of any process of change, but they can be disturbing for some. Bishops and those planning a diocesan assembly of some kind must learn to acknowledge these feelings, both from laypeople and clergy, but not allow the process to be paralysed by them.

❖ Diocesan clergy are very mixed in their attitudes to diocesan projects of this kind. Some are enthusiastic, and a fair proportion will give moderate support, but others are pessimistic or cynical. There may be good reasons; fear of extra burdens and demands; a sense of disillusionment because these processes rarely seem to deliver the kind of instant change that is sometimes hoped for; anger or confusion about the way in which the Church is going; a sense of loss or hurt. It is important to acknowledge these feelings and to see them as opening possibilities for growth. It is also important to note how quickly the negative responses of priests may cause laypeople to become hurt and disillusioned in their turn.

To address this problem, diocesan pastoral processes may need to be preceded by, or accompanied by, dialogue among priests alone. This should not be seen as anti-collaborative; all those involved in collaboration benefit from being able to meet sometimes with others in their own situation. But such dialogue may not be very effective in changing negative outlooks. Often the problem is not the diocesan process as such, but the way in which priests feel about themselves or their ministry, the diocese, the bishop or the Church, and this is much harder to work through.

✤ For an effective diocesan pastoral process, the groundwork and onward planning is probably more important than the large gathering in which it culminates. Both the preparation for a large event, and the follow-up planned, need a great deal of work. In the consultation stage, parish communities learn what consultation really is and how it plays a part in forming decisions. They also discover a common vision, and realise what it means to be part of a diocesan community. In this consultation, expectations and needs can be voiced and adjusted to reality. Skilled local leadership is needed to enable all this to happen.

Pastoral planning for a Church with fewer priests

Most dioceses are likely to face the challenge of having fewer priests in the coming years. There are also fewer religious available for parish work as their numbers decrease and their priorities shift. Some dioceses have already begun consulting and planning, and introducing different patterns of parish and deanery life in order to respond positively to this situation. One particular response which is developing in a number of dioceses is to cluster neighbouring parishes who are then served by one priest, often assisted by deacons, religious and/or lay pastoral workers. This has the advantage of avoiding the closure of parishes and enabling the growth of the parish into greater responsibility.

Inevitably, such discussion and planning includes consideration of collaborative ministry. It is often seen as a fairly straightforward process of assigning more parish responsibilities to laypeople, without much exploration of many of the issues mentioned in this report.

It is tempting to see the situation simply as a matter of re-organising where priests live, the number and times of masses, and similar matters. But in the long run, a parish is more than a mass station, and the larger underlying issues about leadership and parish development matter equally alongside ensuring that the sacraments are celebrated.

There are two sets of issues and questions for dioceses to address, both at parish and deanery level, and at diocesan level:

i   How to consult the people who make up the parish in a way that enables them to become better informed about what is at stake, to think through various possibilities for their own situation, to discern prayerfully what is the best way forward, and to make sound practical plans. The various groups, networks and communities within the parish will need to deepen their understanding of the theology of baptism and of ministry and reflect on their need for leadership and their mission. They will also need to discuss the use of parish funds for salaries, and other practical matters. At the very least, parishes will need skills and formation to help them to explore these questions seriously.

ii How to draw together at diocesan level some strategies to respond to the situation flexibly, taking account of the diversity of situations and people.

These may include finding areas where clusters of parishes will share a priest, other areas which may develop a deanery team, and some parishes which employ a full-time lay 'pastoral life director' or 'pastoral coordinator' with sacramental assistance from a neighbouring priest who acts as canonical pastor. There may also be need for a coordinated approach to the appointment of lay pastoral staff in parishes, and their formation and funding.

It is unavoidable that development of this kind will raise some fundamental questions which are theological as well as pastoral, and not to be taken lightly. Some of these are as follows:

❖ Can a priest be a leader of a parish in a real sense if he does not live there? He may be the canonical pastor, but what happens to the link between presiding at the Eucharist and leading the community?

❖ Can a layperson be a leader of a parish community if he or she cannot preach or preside at sacramental worship? What happens to the bonds of ecclesial communion which ordination symbolises? And what kind of authority does she or he have? What kind of commissioning or recognition is appropriate?

❖ What kind of parish council or parish forum will be effective when there is no resident priest? What kind of authority will it have?

There is no short-cut to resolving the questions raised by the decreasing number of priests. If there are to be ways forward which enable growth and mission, parishes must be helped to find the maturity and leadership to move into new patterns of life. Collaborative ministry is not the only aspect of this process, but it is certainly one essential element.

Full-time pastoral teams

Collaborative ministry is visible in its most concentrated form in full-time pastoral teams where a combination of clergy, laypeople and/or religious work together. This happens in parishes and at diocesan level as well as in pastoral centres and chaplaincy teams. It is an emerging area of church life, and has great vitality but also raises many questions.

Employment and financial questions

❖ There are enormous variations in the conditions of employment for laypeople in pastoral work. Laypeople have to assess an employment situation in legal and moral terms, and find a way of balancing this with their sense of vocation and the desire to minister. They are often willing to work for low salaries, but this does not make it right to employ them at a level which effectively denies them ordinary choices such as the possibility of buying a house.

❖ Those employing them also face a challenge; they must be fair and good employers despite limited resources and changing circumstances. Good employment practice includes proper contracts and job descriptions, induction of staff and policy for staff development and appraisal. Careful thought is also needed about job security. Whilst it is true that this is limited today even in established professional fields, the Church must employ according to criteria drawn from its own social principles, rather than from current economic policies.

✤ As collaborative ministry develops, and dioceses or parishes decide to employ lay pastoral workers, there is need to look seriously at how new income can be generated to cover the costs adequately. This may require new approaches to parish budgeting for mission, and should be taken as seriously as the pastoral and theological development described earlier.

Personal and professional boundaries

✤ Those working in collaborative teams have to recognise personal and professional boundaries and reconcile these with their differing individual situations. As employees, laypeople can expect to have clear boundaries of time, role and place. Clergy and religious often understand and experience such boundaries in different ways. The tensions which can arise are particularly difficult when teams work in residential settings.

✤ Laypeople and priests working together occupy multiple and often conflicting roles. In a parish team, a lay pastoral worker may find herself being parishioner, friend and professional colleague alongside the priest with whom she works, and the priest may likewise look to her in the same ways. Tensions arising from one of these roles can easily be played out inappropriately in the others.

Men and women working together

✤ When men and women collaborate in ministry, they cannot avoid entering the complex territory of understanding the complementarity of masculine and feminine within and between persons. Indeed, the Trinitarian basis of collaboration demands openness to this aspect of relationships. It may be highly charged and can seem risky to some, but it is one of the ways in which collaborative ministry offers a possibility of profound personal and spiritual growth.

✤ More practically, it is increasingly recognised that men and women characteristically have different ways of communicating and can easily misunderstand each others' needs and intentions. Teams need to work very hard at how they communicate, and enable different members to take responsibility for what they think and feel.

Interface with the parish and wider Church

✤ Teams working within a parish or deanery have to take great care about their relationship to the communities they serve. The team can sometimes seem very exclusive, and can tend to reproduce something parallel to the clericalism of old by excluding the wider community from decision-making or formulation of vision.

... collaborative ministry offers a possibility of profound personal and spiritual growth.

43

✤ Teams sometimes face tensions arising from how members feel about the wider Church. Some may project their need to be looked after onto the Church through the team, and others may express their need to rebel and have autonomy. In others, there may be feelings of anger, hurt and frustration associated with the Church which further complicate collaborative ministry.

Collaborative ministry teams have to negotiate these tensions with care, sensitivity and clear ecclesial vision. They also have to ensure that their internal struggles to grow as a team do not absorb so much energy that their broader purpose suffers.

Conclusion

Some people regard collaborative ministry as an option. Others see it as a necessity, an unavoidable aspect of what the Church essentially it. Some see it as a process of mild evolution, a gentle adjustment of how work is done, and others as a radical re-shaping of all that the Church is.

It is not possible, or desirable, to exclude any of these views, nor to prove any one of them definitively correct. The very basis of collaboration, the reality and desire for communion between us because of our sharing in God's own life, demands that we include, accept and value different paces of growth and varying convictions.

Ultimately, what matters is that we live communion in the Church, drawing life from each other in and through our relationship. If the Church is a communion of love, we will be better able to build a civilisation of love, communicating to our world through what we are, the deepest truths about persons and society.

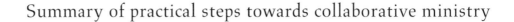

Summary of practical steps towards collaborative ministry

At parish level: what priests and parish leaders can do

❖ Develop a parish pastoral council or forum, or a pastoral planning group, and ensure that it has appropriate theological, spiritual and practical formation. Think out how to express its relationship with the wider parish community.

❖ Develop a parish ministries plan; encourage ministry groups such as the readers, or the RCIA team, or bereavement ministers, to arrange their own formation and recruit new members; establish a policy about how long ministries are held for, and how they are recognised and celebrated. Invite the parish to make sure that those involved in ministries include as many different kinds of people as possible.

❖ Enable various groups within the parish to learn how to carry out effective consultation; discuss and try out different ways of decision-making in these groups and especially in parish pastoral councils. Encourage reflection on the best ways to make various decisions affecting the parish, and agree the criteria to use.

❖ Engage as many people as possible in the parish in thinking about the future, including ways the parish can continue to grow if there is no resident priest; discuss ideas such as parish pastoral assistants and think through the practical and theological implications.

❖ Look for opportunities to reflect on the culture of the parish and identify some special events in which the parish experience of collaboration can be symbolised and celebrated.

At diocesan level: what bishops can do

❖ Give consistent encouragement to collaborative ministry in teaching and ministry.

❖ Encourage those responsible for formation of all kinds to give some priority to the attitudes, understanding and skills needed for collaborative ministry.

❖ Consider how appointments of priests to parishes are made; see whether this can be done in ways that strengthen the sense of collaboration between priests and bishop; examine ways of avoiding transition problems which undermine the progress towards collaboration in parishes.

❖ Develop policy about the employment of lay pastoral workers, including guidelines to ensure fair employment practice and financial strategies where appropriate.

❖ Encourage or extend planning for the future, addressing the theological and practical issues that will arise when there are fewer priests.

Background and terms of reference for the working party

In 1992, the National Conference of Priests took collaborative ministry as the theme for its annual meeting. Following its discussion, it asked the Bishops' Conference to set up a working party to see how the growth of collaborative ministry could be encouraged, particularly at diocesan level. The Bishops' Conference agreed to this request in November 1992, and the terms of reference and membership of the working party were later approved by its Standing Committee. The first meeting took place in September 1993.

The terms of reference for the working party

1 Aim and objectives

   i   The working party will identify some possible and practical steps to develop appropriate patterns of collaborative ministry at parish, diocesan and national level, building upon existing experience and reflecting a renewed vision of the Church for the future.

   ii To do this, the working party will:

- describe what collaborative ministry means in practice.

- listen to existing experience of collaborative ministry in various situations.

- identify some of the factors which assist the growth of collaborative ministry and some factors which block its development.

- examine some of the practical factors which influence the need for collaboration and some of the implications which follow from these.

- outline some relevant theological principles which will need to influence future patterns of ministry and leadership in the Church, and identify some of the implications.

   iii In the light of these reflections, the working party will develop proposals about possible and practical steps that can be taken in various areas of Church life.

   iv The working party cannot develop strategies for the whole Church or for all aspects of its life. It will need to identify some key areas in which it will pursue the aim and objectives described above. It will also clarify at an early stage what kind of outcome it aims to produce, and to whom its work may best be offered by the Bishops' Conference.

2 Style of working and membership

The working party should be a small group with about twelve members. Its task is analytical and reflective, in order to offer ideas to assist the growth of the Church. It will need to listen to the experience of particular individuals or groups, and therefore may occasionally have a larger meeting.

How the work was carried out

The working party has met on eight occasions. It has twelve members, six men and six women including a seminary rector, a diocesan special needs adviser, a member of a religious order, two parish pastoral assistants, two parish priests, a diocesan bishop, a diocesan pastoral council secretary, a psychotherapist and two members of the Bishops' Conference staff. The members were invited to take part on the basis of their experience, rather than to represent any particular group.

Through its members, the working party has listened in depth to parish, diocesan and national level experience, as well as perspectives from seminaries and other particular sectors of pastoral work. It has not attempted any large-scale consultation other than through the networks and experience of its members. The input for discussion at each meeting has come from a series of short papers presented by the members of the working party, together with a certain amount of background reading. A number of consultants were invited to comment on the draft report as the work concluded.

The terms of reference acknowledge the limitations of a working party of this kind *(see 1.iv above)*. The working party took this advice very seriously. It began its first meeting by identifying some key areas, planning the timescale for its work and setting a deadline for completion. It has also kept in mind the primary purpose of offering its work first of all to the Bishops' Conference.

Membership of the working party and consultants

Dorothy Bell RSCJ	Southwark Diocese AIDS Adviser
Mgr Philip Carroll	General Secretary, Bishops' Conference
Clare Connors	Adviser for people with disabilities: Southwark Diocese
Fr Paul Crowe	Former Parish Priest, now Director of Ireneus Centre
Pauline Farrell	Organisation Consultant and Counsellor
Mary Grisdale	Brentwood Diocesan Pastoral Council Secretary
Bishop Crispian Hollis	Portsmouth Diocese
Pat Jones	Assistant General Secretary, Bishops' Conference
Sorie Kajue	Parish Pastoral Worker, Salford Diocese
Mgr Pat McKinney	Rector, Oscott Seminary
Fr Brian O'Sullivan	Parish Priest, former Chairman of National Conference of Priests
Liz Wilson	Parish Pastoral Worker

Consultants

Vicky Cosstick	Pastoral Director, Allen Hall Seminary
Elizabeth Ridley	Pastoral Worker, Northampton Diocese
Fr Michael Campbell	Secretary, Bishops' Conference Theology Committee
Cecily Boulding OP	Lecturer, Ushaw College, Member of Bishops' Conference Theology Committee
Fr Jim O'Keefe	Secretary, Bishops' Conference Social Welfare Committee
Fr Roderick Strange	Chairman, National Conference of Priests
Fr Mervin Smith	Secretary, National Conference of Priests

List of books and documents quoted

Papal, Council and Synod Documents

Mystici Corporis: Pius XII 1943

Christifideles Laici: Pope John Paul II 1989 (CFL)

Lumen Gentium: Vatican Council II: The Conciliar and Post Conciliar Documents (LG)

Apostolicam Actuositatem: Vatican Council II: The Conciliar and Post-Conciliar
Documents (AA)

Evangelii Nuntiandi: Pope Paul VI 1975 (EN)

Pastores Dabo Vobis: Pope John Paul II 1992 (PDV)

The Extraordinary Synod: Message and Final Report 1986

*Letter to the Bishops of the Catholic Church on some aspects of the Church
understood as communion:* 1992 (CDF)

Catechism of the Catholic Church 1994 (CCC)

Other books and documents

Reflections: Bishops' Conference of England and Wales, Briefing October 1993

The Motherhood of the Church: Henri de Lubac SJ 1982

The Parish Project: Vicky Cosstick, Declan Lang, Damian Lundy and John O'Shea.
National Project of Religious Education and Catechesis. Rejoice Publications.

Material for study and discussion

The following outlines for study and discussion will help those who wish to explore the contents and implications of this report together. They could be used by groups such as pastoral councils, groups of eucharistic ministers or catechists, parish teams, deacons or seminarians in training, chaplaincy teams and others.

The first three outlines will be particularly helpful for groups who are still moving towards collaborative ministry. The second three outlines are more appropriate for those with experience of collaborative ministry.

When using outlines 1, 3, 4 and 5, a flip-chart is needed. Outlines 2, 4 and 6 need sections of the report or other material copying during the meeting.

Each outline is intended for a discussion period of around an hour and a half. It is important that there is a leader for the discussion who has read the material and prepared what is needed. The leader should also adapt the material to suit the needs of the group. Some groups may ask one of their members to lead. Others may invite someone to come and work with them to use the material.

Each outline has four sections:

DESCRIBE AND EXPLORE   *(15 minutes)*

Ways to invite people to identify and explore their own experience and understanding.

LISTEN AND REFLECT   *(45 minutes)*

Ways to invite people to reflect on new ideas or deepen their understanding.

ACT DIFFERENTLY   *(15 minutes)*

Ways to invite people to think about the implications of what they have discussed
for the way we live and work together.

PRAY AND CELEBRATE   *(15 minutes)*

Some suggestions for scriptural reflection, prayer and celebration.

THEMES

There are six outlines:

> Language and limitations
>
> Exploring the Trinity
>
> Parish leadership - whose task?
>
> Why choose collaborative ministry?
>
> Celebrating collaboration
>
> Collaboration, conflict and growth

Language and limitations

The aim of this session is to enable people to think about the language we use and the attitudes it contains and communicates, and to deepen their understanding of some important aspects of who we are and how we relate to each other in the Church.

DESCRIBE AND EXPLORE

✤ Invite the group to list the words that we use to name each other; and write these up on a flipchart e.g.

The laity	The baptised	Priests	The hierarchy

Discuss these; ask people to say which they like, and which they dislike, and why. How do they overlap? What connotations do they have? Do they help to bring us together or do they get in the way? Which terms are preferable? Does it matter which terms are used?

✤ Then write up some expressions for collaborative ministry:

Collaborative ministry	Working in partnership
Working as a team	Shared responsibility
Communion in mission	

Invite people to say which they like, and why.
Are there any differences between these? If so, what?

LISTEN AND REFLECT

✤ The report says in the introduction:

It is not possible to move very far forward into collaborative ministry without realising that language matters. The way we speak about each other reflects and forms attitudes and relationships. (p.10)

Does the group agree? What language do members find difficult, and why? What changes would they like to see?

✤ Write up another list of words:

Equal terms and equal valuing of people	Mutual trust and recognition
Authority	Leadership
Power	

Ask the group to say what they think each of these terms means. Then get someone to find a sentence or two from pp.22-29 which explains each word, and discuss these. How can we help each other, and others in the Church, to understand these terms more fully? Is there a gap between what these words imply, and the reality we experience? What can be done about it?

ACT DIFFERENTLY

❖ Look back at the lists of words: Ask each member of the group to choose one word that we need to understand better and put into practice in the Church, and to suggest how this might be done.

PRAYER AND CELEBRATION

❖ Ask someone to read 1 Peter 2:9-10

> But you are a chosen race,
> a royal priesthood,
> a holy nation,
> God's own people,
> in order that you may proclaim the mighty acts
> of him who called you out of darkness
> into his marvellous light.
>
> Once you were not a people,
> but now you are God's people;
> once you has not received mercy,
> but now you have received mercy.

Invite people to reflect and pray with these words; what do they say to us about ourselves and our relationships with each other?

Invite people to share reflections or prayers.

❖ Finish by reading together the prayer below.

> Spirit of God
> Lord and Giver of Life,
> moving between us and around
> like wind or water or fire;
> breathe into us your freshness that we may awake;
> cleanse our vision that we may see more clearly;
> kindle our senses that we may feel more sharply;
> and give us the courage to live
> as you would have us live
> through Jesus Christ our Lord.

From *A Matter of Life and Death* John V Taylor, SCM Press 1986

Exploring the Trinity

The aim of this session is to invite people to discover what it means for our lives and relation-ships to believe in the Trinity, and to begin to see how collaborative ministry is one way of living out this central part of our faith.

DESCRIBE AND EXPLORE

❖ Invite people to recall the images and ideas about the Trinity that they have grown up with, and share these with the group.

❖ Suggest that as adults, we need to look afresh at this central doctrine and explore its meaning. Ask people to spend a few minutes alone, thinking about these questions:

> How do you understand the Trinity?
>
> How do you see the relationships between Father, Son and Spirit?
>
> What kind of images capture the relationships?

After a while, invite them to discuss their responses with two or three other people, and then invite some feedback to the whole group.

LISTEN AND REFLECT

❖ Look together at some texts. It will be helpful if these have been copied onto a page beforehand; from the *Catechism of the Catholic Church* 234, 255, 1877; from this report pp 19-20; or the following section of the Athanasian Creed

> And so the Father is God, the Son is God and the Holy Ghost is God.
> And yet there are not three Gods, but one God.
> And in this Trinity none is afore, or after the other; none is greater,
>   or less than another;
> But the whole three persons are co-eternal together and co-equal.
> So that in all things, as is aforesaid, the unity in Trinity and the Trinity in unity is to
>   be worshipped.
> *The Athanasian Creed*

Invite the group to explore what these tell us about God's life, and what they tell us about ourselves and our different relationships.

ACT DIFFERENTLY

Ask the group to discuss this question:

> What are the implications of believing in the Trinity
> - for our personal lives?
> - for our life together as the Church?
> - for our society?

PRAYER AND CELEBRATION

✤ Ask someone to read John 17: 20-25, and invite the group to sit prayerfully with these words for a few minutes.

✤ Invite the group to recall the times when Jesus speaks about the Father, or about the Spirit; look at some texts such as John 15:26, John 16:12-16, Luke 10:21-23, Luke 11:13, Luke 12:30-32, Mark 14:32-36, Matthew 3:16-17, John 1:1-5, 14, 18.

What glimpses of the Trinity do we get from the gospels?

Invite people to choose one text which draws them or fascinates them, and say why.

✤ Say or sing together St. Patrick's Breastplate.

I bind unto myself today
the strong name of the Trinity:
By invocation of the same,
The Three in One and One in Three.

I bind unto myself today
The power of God to hold and lead:
His eye to watch, his might to stay,
His ear to hearken to my need,

The wisdom of my God to teach,
His hand to guide, his shield to ward;
The word of God to give me speech,
His heavenly host to be my guard.

I bind unto myself the name,
The strong name of the Trinity;
By invocation of the same,
The Three in One and One in Three,
Of whom all nature hath creation;
Eternal Father, Spirit, Word:
Praise to the God of my salvation:
Salvation is of Christ the Lord.

… or use a modern Celtic prayer:

Enable us, Father, Creator,
To walk in your light
To work by your might
To long for your sight.

Enable us, Jesus, Redeemer,
To look for your healing
To know your appealing
To live for your revealing.

Enable us, Spirit, Strengthener,
With power in your confiding
With peace through your providing
With presence through your abiding.

Enable us,
Trinity
In Unity,
Unity
In Trinity.
Enable us, O God.

From *Power Lines: Celtic Prayers about Work*
by David Adam. Triangle Books.

Parish leadership – whose task?

The aim of this session is to help groups to explore what leadership in a parish involves, and to reflect on the link between leadership and priestly ministry, and also to consider how the baptised can share in leadership.

DESCRIBE AND EXPLORE

✤ Ask the group to consider and discuss who provides leadership in their parish. What are the essential aspects of leadership in a parish?

✤ Describe a situation in which three parishes share a priest, who lives in one of the parishes, but 'looks after' all three. In one of the parishes a permanent deacon is the main point of contact; in another, there is a parish council, but they are not used to being without a priest. Ask the group to consider these questions:

> How would you feel if you were a parishioner in this cluster?
>
> What would be the main problems that could arise?
>
> How would you feel if you were the priest?
>
> What structures are needed to make it work?

LISTEN AND REFLECT

✤ Invite people to think about the theological questions which arise when laypeople fulfil the main leadership role in a parish, with a part-time or visiting priest. Look at pages 36-42 of this report, and focus on these questions:

> How can a priest be a leader of a parish community in a real sense if he does not live or work there in any substantial way? He may be the canonical pastor, but what happens to the link between presiding at the Eucharist and leading the community?
>
> Can a layperson be a leader of a parish community if he or she cannot preach or preside at sacramental worship? What happens to the bonds of ecclesial communion which ordination symbolises? What kind of authority does she or he have, and what kind of commissioning or recognition is appropriate?
>
> What kind of parish council or forum will be effective where there is no resident priest? What kind of authority will it have?

✤ Make a list of other issues that emerge. Write these on a flipchart, and discuss them. These questions may help.

> Do we need to renew our understanding of priesthood, in order to respond positively to situations where there are fewer priests?
>
> Do we need to take baptism more seriously? What attitudes need to change?

ACT DIFFERENTLY

❖ What needs to be done in your parish to help people to think more deeply about these matters?

❖ How can we find ways for more people to share in leadership in the parish? What structures, or formation, is needed?

PRAYER AND CELEBRATION

❖ Ask two people to read aloud two gospel stories:

Jesus washing the feet of his disciples: John 13:1-17
The woman who anoints Jesus with precious ointment: Mark 14:3-9

Invite people to pray quietly with these stories for some minutes.

Then invite them to share their reflections;

What does each story tell us about leadership? About ministry?

What does each story tell us about relationships between people who follow Jesus?

❖ Finish by reading the prayer below:

Jesus our brother,
you followed the necessary path
and were broken on our behalf.
May we neither cling to our pain
where it is futile,
nor refuse to embrace the cost
when it is required of us;
that in losing our selves for your sake,
we may be brought to new life.
Amen.
From *All Desires Known* by Janet Morley.

Why choose collaborative ministry?

The aim of this session is to help people to realise that collaborative ministry does not happen by accident; to grow fully, it needs to be chosen in a definite way; and to help people to explore what is distinctive about collaborative ministry.

DESCRIBE AND EXPLORE

❖ Ask people in the group to discuss this question in two's or three's;

> Would you say that in your ministry situation, you have chosen collaborative ministry in a definite way? How and why did you choose it? How does it change your ways of working? And if not, why not?

Invite some feedback.

❖ Ask the group to brainstorm on this question:

> What is distinctive about collaborative ministry, that makes it a new way of working together?

Write up responses on a flipchart.

LISTEN AND REFLECT

❖ Give out a page with the five descriptions of collaborative ministry from Part II p.17 of this report. Ask the group to comment; do they agree with all of these? Which of these seems closest to their own convictions or experience? Which is most challenging?

❖ Invite the group to divide into two's and three's and ask each cluster to write their own single sentence summing up what is distinctive or new about collaborative ministry. After fifteen minutes or so, invite the groups to share their sentences and discuss them together.

ACT DIFFERENTLY

❖ Ask people to identify two or three ways that the parish or group or team needs to grow, to become more collaborative.

PRAYER AND CELEBRATION

✤ Read aloud the following two passages:

> Do not remember the former things
> or consider the things of old.
> I am about to do a new thing;
> how it springs forth, do you not perceive it?
> I will make a way in the wilderness
> and rivers in the desert.
> The wild animals will honour me,
> the jackals and the ostriches;
> for I give water in the wilderness,
> rivers in the desert,
> to give drink to my chosen people,
> the people whom I formed for myself
> so that they might declare my praise.
>
> Isaiah 43:18-21

> Sing, O barren one who did not bear:
> burst into song and shout,
> you who have not been in labour!
> For the children of the desolate woman will be more
> than the children of her that is married, says the Lord.
> Enlarge the site of your tent,
> and let the curtains of your habitations be stretched out;
> do not hold back; lengthen your cords
> and strengthen your stakes.
> For you will spread out to the right and to the left,
> and your descendants will possess the nations
> and will settle the desolate towns.
>
> Isaiah 54:1-3.

Invite the group to share their reflections; what light do these passages shed on collaborative ministry? What images do people find powerful?

✤ Finish by reading the prayer below:

> Holy God
> whose presence is known
> in the structures we build
> and in their collapse;
> establish in us a community of hope,
> not to contain your mystery,
> but to be led beyond security
> into your sacred space,
> through Jesus Christ, Amen.
>
> From *All Desires Known* by Janet Morley.

Celebrating collaboration

The aim of this session is to help the group to become aware of how to support and strengthen collaborative ministry by making it visible in liturgical and sacramental life, and by finding new symbols and rituals which help to celebrate and deepen the experience of collaboration.

DESCRIBE AND EXPLORE

✤ Invite people to list the ways in which laypeople play a visible part in the celebration of liturgy and the sacraments in the parish. Write these on a flip chart. Check that the list includes the following, if appropriate:

> readers, collectors, altar servers, cantors, children's catechists, lay leaders of Eucharistic services or funerals, Eucharistic ministers, those who welcome people at the door etc.

Are there any ways that laypeople could be active which have not yet been developed?

✤ What difference does it make to people when they take on a ministry in the parish? Does it change their own attitudes to faith and the Church?

✤ Look at the list of people involved in liturgical ministries in your parish:

Overall, what is the balance of women and men, young and old, different ethnic backgrounds, people with disabilities?

Does the balance show that the Church is for all? How could it be better?

LISTEN AND REFLECT

✤ Give people a copy of p.32 on *Liturgical Celebration*. Ask them to read it and underline the points they think are most important or most needed in your parish. Then discuss these: why are these important? What difference could they make to the parish? What kind of practical steps forward could be taken?

✤ Invite people to be creative; what kind of new gestures, or symbols, or ways of arranging liturgy, would celebrate collaboration and help it grow? Here are two examples:

> When Fr. Gerry came to our parish, there was an induction mass. The dean presented him to the parish, and we prayed for him, but we also had an exchange of gifts to welcome him. Some of us from the parish gave him gifts to symbolise what we are like as a parish, our history and strengths and needs. We gave him a sweatshirt with the school logo, because the school is very important to us, and the parish council minutes book, and a box of biscuits to show we hope he settles here. He gave us a South American blanket, from his work there, and a picture of Archbishop Romero for the Church, and a candle, to symbolise prayer. It felt like agreeing to share our lives, priest and people together. It was a good start.
>
> We have a parish ministries renewal Sunday. All the people who are readers or Eucharistic ministers come, and some are stepping down, and new people are beginning. We ask the retiring ministers to say something about their experience and to pray for the new ones, and we ask the new ones to give a small gift - a prayer card, or small icon - to those who are finishing. We try to make sure that everyone gets a chance.

✤ Invite the group to discuss what could be done at Confirmation, or what could be done to celebrate the work of the parish pastoral council?

ACT DIFFERENTLY

✤ Ask each person to think of one practical step which could help the parish to celebrate collaboration and make it more visible. Discuss how to act on these.

PRAYER AND CELEBRATION

✤ Read one or more of the following scripture passages:

John 12:12-16 – The entry of Jesus into Jerusalem on a donkey.

John 13:1-15 – The washing of feet.

Acts 2:44-47 – The way the first disciples lived and celebrated their faith.

Invite the group to reflect on the symbolic actions in each of these stories.
What do they say to us? What response do they evoke?

Invite the members of the group each to describe a symbol of collaborative ministry that they would like to offer to the group

✤ Finish with a time of silent prayer, and either say a closing prayer together:

> O God our mystery
> you bring us to life
> call us to freedom,
> and move between us with love.
> May we so participate
> in the dance of your Trinity
> that our lives may resonate with you,
> now and for ever. Amen.
>
> From *All desires known* by Janet Morley

or sing or say a suitable song

Here in this place, new light is streaming,
now is the darkness vanished away.
See, in this space, our fears and our dreamings,
brought here to you in the light of this day.
Gather us in the lost and forsaken,
gather us in the blind and the lame;
call to us now, and we shall awaken,
we shall arise at the sound of your name.

We are the young – our lives are a mystery,
we are the old – who yearn for your face,
we have been sung throughout all of history,
called to be light to the whole human race.
Gather us in the rich and the haughty,
gather us in the proud and the strong;
give us a heart so meek and so lowly,
give us the courage to enter the song.

Here we will take the wine and the water,
here we will take the bread of new birth,
here we shall call your sons and your daughters,
call us anew to be salt for the earth.
Give us to drink the wine of compassion,
give us to eat the bread that is you;
nourish us well and teach us to fashion,
lives that are holy and hearts that are true.

Not in the dark of buildings confining,
not in some heaven light years away, but
here in this place, the new light is shining,
now is the Kingdom, now is the day.
Gather us in and hold us for ever,
gather us and make us your own;
gather us in all peoples together,
fire of love in our flesh and our bone.

Marty Haugen *Gather us in*

Collaboration, conflict and growth

The aim of this session is to help those involved in collaborative ministry to reflect on their experience and to identify the change asked of them by collaboration.

DESCRIBE AND EXPLORE

✤ Ask the group to spend a few minutes reflecting individually on these questions;

> In what ways have you changed through your experience of collaboration?
>
> What barriers to collaboration have you experienced in others, or in yourself?
>
> What causes conflict between collaborating partners, and what helps growth to happen?

Then spend some time taking each question in turn, and listening to people's answers.

LISTEN AND REFLECT

Either

✤ Look at the sections of the report *Openness to Change* p.29 and *Spirituality* p.35 and ask the group to respond.

> Does the report echo your experience?
>
> Does it offer any helpful perspectives?
>
> How do you see the link between spirituality and collaborative ministry?

Or

✤ Look at the sections of the report on *Learning to deal with conflict* p.30 and *Barriers to growth* p.34, and ask the group to discuss these.

> Does the report echo your experience?
>
> Does it offer any helpful perspectives?
>
> How can collaborative partners learn to deal with conflict? What help do they need?

ACT DIFFERENTLY

✤ Invite the group to discuss what kinds of support or formation would help those involved in collaboration to grow through experience.

What kinds of skills do we need to learn?

What kind of opportunities would help deepen a spirituality of collaboration?

Plan one further formation opportunity based on what has emerged in these discussions.

PRAYER AND CELEBRATION

❖ Read together 2 Cor 4: 7-15

> But we have this treasure in clay jars
> so that it might be made clear
> that this extraordinary power comes from God
> and does not come from us.
> We are afflicted in every way, but not crushed;
> perplexed, but not driven to despair;
> persecuted but not forsaken;
> struck down, but not destroyed;
> always carrying in the body the death of Jesus,
> so that the life of Jesus may also be made visible in our bodies.
> For while we live,
> we are always being given up to death for Jesus' sake,
> so that the life of Jesus might be made visible in our mortal flesh.
> So death is at work in us, but life in you.
> But just as we have the same spirit of faith that is in accordance
> with the scripture - 'I believed, and so I spoke' -
> we also believe, and so we speak,
> because we know that the one who raised the Lord Jesus
> will raise us also with Jesus
> and bring us with you into his presence.
> Yes, everything is for your sake,
> so that grace, as it extends to more and more people,
> may increase thanksgiving, to the glory of God.

and look together at this poem by RS Thomas

> When we are weak, we are
> strong. When our eyes close
> on the world, then somewhere
> within us the bush
> burns. When we are poor
> and aware of the inadequacy
> of our table, it is to that
> uninvited the guest comes.
> R S Thomas: *Counterpoint*. Bloodaxe Books.

Spend some time in silence, then invite people to share responses, reflections and prayers.

❖ Finish by saying an Our Father.